COOKBOOK FOR AWAKENING
CORE TEACHINGS FROM RAM DASS

Dedication

This book is a testament to the power of unconditional love—specifically the love that Neem Karoli Baba (Maharaj-ji) showered on Ram Dass during their first encounter in 1967. Ram Dass has shared that love without any expectations over these many years and to that intention we dedicate this book.

INGREDIENTS

  5   Introduction

  6   Awareness

12   Meditation

18   Unconditional Love

26   Relationship

32   Service and Compassionate Action

41   Credits

For specially curated video and audio talks from Ram Dass that will illuminate the core teachings in this book go to ramdass.org/cookbook

INTRODUCTION TO COOKBOOK FOR AWAKENING

Over the past five decades, the heart wisdom of Ram Dass has been an oasis for so many who are seeking new perspective and direction in their spiritual lives.

The time he spent with his guru, Neem Karoli Baba, set him on a path of service, and inspired him to share his practices with anyone seeking spiritual guidance. These practices help us live in a way that awakens our hearts and minds, and alleviates suffering in ourselves and others. They help us to bridge the gap between our egos and our souls – who we think we are, and who we really are.

With this in mind, we decided to create a collection of teachings on topics that are some of the key ingredients for awakening. These are topics that, in our experience, most resonated with people who are looking to inhabit "be here now" in a truly authentic way.

This scrapbook contains some of Ram Dass' most potent teachings on awareness, meditation, relationships, unconditional love, and service/compassionate action, which reflect his journey over these many years. Our hope is that you will not only find truth, wisdom, and joy in these pages, but you will share what you find with your family and friends.

Thank you for bringing this Cookbook for Awakening into your home, and your heart.

Namaste,

Raghu Markus
Director, Love Serve Remember Foundation (RamDass.org)

Gandhi

God demands nothing less than complete self-surrender as the price for the only real freedom that is worth having. And when a person thus loses him/her self, he (she) immediately finds himself (her) in the service of all that lives. It becomes her delight & recreation. She is a new person never weary of spending herself in the service of God's creation

AWARENESS

THE FLASHLIGHT OF AWARENESS

Awareness is like a flashlight that illuminates the phenomena constantly presenting itself in our lives. So when your knee itches – flash. You suddenly think of the latest tragedy in Syria – flash. You are suddenly aware of the sun rising – flash. It's just going flash, flash, flash…

You can most easily watch your consciousness when you're just waking up in the morning. It's fun because you're moving in and out of planes until the thought comes, "I need to go to the bathroom." It sort of stands out like a thought in space. It's, "I need to go to the bathroom." It's nothing personal, just the expression of that need. Then another one like, "I could sleep ten more minutes." Then they really start, "It's warm in that corner; I've gotta make that phone call; gotta do the laundry; Oh, I wish I could smell coffee." On and on it goes and you start like a trip-hammer all day long, "Think me – think me – think me – I'm real, think me – think me – gotta think of me and hey, have you thought of me?"

The thoughts are very fast, so it all seems solid, but it's actually linear. Isn't that far out? You spend a moment keeping yourself erect so that you can ignore that and do something else, but it's still happening. All these incredible adjustment mechanisms. And then when you see that there is the flashlight flashing on all of these things, you realize the flashlight can't flash on itself, can you hear the predicament?

The question is how could you possibly examine whether or not you are the flashlight instead of all the phenomena the flashlight flashes on, including yourself. The thought of "who I think I am" is something the flashlight flashes on.

And what are the qualities of the flashlight? It's just awareness.

AWARENESS AND ATTACHMENT

If awareness is like a flashlight, then what it shines brightest on is our desires. So that means the game is to extricate your awareness from attachment to those desires. The desires go on, they're there. The only point is you are no longer identified with those desires.

You say, "Well, I can't imagine how that could be." But you're doing it all the time. Very often you are performing behavior that is satisfying various needs on your part and yet your awareness is not caught in being the actor, or being the getter of gratification. Yet you're doing it.

For example, many of you drive cars. I'll bet many of you find yourself hurtling through space, hopefully in a car, guiding three, four thousand pounds of metal while making incredibly complex decisions about centripetal and centrifugal forces, inertia, and all kinds of complex physics laws. All the time you might be tuning the radio, looking out for police, thinking about where you're going, remembering where you've been. You never even think about driving anymore. When you're new, you think about driving. Then it goes into what we call base brain and it's just sort of happening. It's a very complex behavior.

You say, "Well, driving is one thing, but really there are important things I've got to think about." Is that true? Is there any drama in life that is so seductive that it pulls you in where you lose your space? Where you lose that part of you that is not identified with the desire?

That's what happens in the process of awakening. At first, you awaken out of your attachments, and then the attachments pull you back in, and you are back wanting, desiring, fearing, hoping, yearning, etcetera. And then, as the process goes on, you start to develop that spaciousness of awareness, that presence, that open-heartedness, even as you are having these desires.

For a long time, however, a desire will take over your consciousness. Ouspensky, who was one of the students of Gurdjieff, wrote a book called *In Search of the Miraculous*. He advocated a method called self-remembering in which you develop a witness, which is another part of you that notices what you are doing. He describes how he would experiment with himself. He'd say, "Ouspensky is setting out for a walk. Ouspensky is walking down the street. Ouspensky is turning left." And he would be watching.

"Ouspensky is lifting his left foot. Ouspensky is lifting his right foot." He was watching all of it, witnessing it. Then he saw his tobacconist shop and remembered he needed pipe tobacco, and he lost it completely. Two days later he remembered he was doing an experiment. He went under completely into the desire; the desire took him over.

You can all feel that. You can feel where you're going along very spacious, very free, very loving, very open, and then something comes up that pulls you completely into your attachment. Your fear, your yearning, your rejection, your anxiety, your doubt, your concern, your something. And the process of using your life experiences as a vehicle for awakening is to sit with that process. You babysit this process in yourself so that you see yourself get stuck, and then you see yourself come up for air. And you begin to notice what it is that sticks to you, where you are clinging, which things grab your awareness.

EMOTIONS AND AWARENESS

Think about the relation of emotions to the constant state of awareness. Awareness is like the sky, and emotions are like birds that are crossing the sky, they come and they go. For example, say you're overwhelmed with negative emotions; the sky is full of menacing looking birds. The un-awakened response to that would simply be, "I'm depressed." The awakened response is more like, "Dig this depression! Look at all those cool birds!" It's just a different place that you're saying it from. The interesting thing is the fact that you even noticed the depression means there's a little part of you that isn't depressed, because who's noticing?

So you begin to play with that little flicker of consciousness. At first, it's just the tiniest little thread. It's like the story of the guy in the tower and his wife wants to save him, so she sends a bug up the tower with a thread hitched to its leg. Then when he gets the thread she attaches a string to it, and then a rope to the string, and he keeps pulling up. Finally, he climbs down the rope and escapes. It all started with a tiny thread.

And that's really all you've got at first is just the tiniest thread of awareness amidst all these raging emotions and thoughts and desires and fears and hopes. There's just this little thread of it, but it's persistent, and pretty soon it starts to permeate everything.

> *The witness is your centering device. It guides the work you do on yourself.*

CULTIVATING THE WITNESS

One way to get free of attachment is to cultivate the witness consciousness, to become a neutral observer of your own life. The witness place inside you is simple awareness, the part of you that is aware of everything — just noticing, watching, not judging, just being present, being here now.

The witness is actually another level of consciousness. The witness coexists alongside your normal consciousness as another layer of awareness, as the part of you that is awakening. Humans have this unique ability to be in two states of consciousness at once. Witnessing yourself is like directing the beam of a flashlight back at itself. In any experience — sensory, emotional, or conceptual — there's the experience, the sensory or emotional or thought data, and there's your awareness of it. That's the witness, the awareness, and you can cultivate that awareness in the garden of your being.

The witness is your awareness of your own thoughts, feelings, and emotions. Witnessing is like waking up in the morning and then looking in the mirror and noticing yourself — not judging or criticizing, just neutrally observing the quality of being awake. That process of stepping back takes you out of being submerged in your experiences and thoughts and sensory input and into self-awareness.

Along with that self-awareness comes the subtle joy of just being here, alive, enjoying being present in this moment. Eventually, floating in that subjective awareness, the objects of awareness dissolve, and you will come into the spiritual Self, the Atman, which is pure consciousness, joy, compassion, the One.

The witness is your centering device. It guides the work you do on yourself. Once you understand that there is a place in you that is not attached, you can extricate yourself from attachments. Pretty much everything we notice in the universe is a reflection of our attachments.

Jesus warned us, *"Lay not up for yourselves treasures upon earth, where moth and rust doth corrupt . . . For where your treasure is, there will your heart be also."* Desire creates your universe; that's just the way it works. So your first job is to work on yourself. The greatest thing you can do for another human being is to get your own house in order and find your true spiritual heart.

EXPLORING AWARENESS THROUGH SUFFERING

In order to be able to cultivate awareness of the intuitive heart, you have to finally come to terms with things like suffering and death.

Many of us respond to them with denial, because it's just too much, and you close the heart to protect yourself, with despair. To that extent you are not able to be with what is, and there's a part of you that is locked in, closed off from the universe, so you're saying, "I wanna be everything. We are all one except for *that*. *That's* too horrible. I can't bear *that*." And what the game deals with is bearing the unbearable. "I can't bear it." Right, well, here we are. Now what? Explore where "I can't bear it" comes from. It's the idea that "I'll crack open if my heart breaks." Well, if your heart doesn't break you'll starve to death. That's your choice. Spiritually starve. That's your choice.

I'd rather have my heartbreak again and again and again, moment by moment, because then I am alive in the situation. I'm getting fed and I'm feeding and we are together. So that when I work with somebody who's terminally ill, that's an interesting moment, because the immensity of their suffering can make me pull back to protect myself from the pain of fully getting into what it must be like to be a young woman or a young man dying of AIDS. I mean, think about the many levels of suffering in there, or causes of suffering: social ostracism, opportunistic illness, lack of emotional and economic support, I mean, thousands of things. Loss of dreams, loss of energies, loss, loss, loss, loss, loss.

That's a heavy storyline, and it's really hard not to get stuck in it. For the person and for you. But if I get stuck in it, if you are the person dying of AIDS, I have just trapped you with my mind in that identity. And you have many identities. A lot of people that are ill often are afraid to tell anybody because they feel that after that everybody would see them just as somebody with cancer, or somebody with AIDS, and they will lose their identity.

Well, it's just another identity, and you've gotta be ready to lose them all for it to become interesting. Even the ones you were holding onto thinking that's who you were. But I go into the room and I can see where my consciousness is immediately by how much I glom onto the storyline and can't bring my awareness back into the spaciousness that sees it as another storyline and understands the mystery of the universe, because that's the way you deal with the suffering.

What you're saying is, "My rational mind can't figure out why there's suffering in the world." You're saying, "If my rational mind were God, it wouldn't make suffering." But it isn't! And you don't even know, 'cause the rational mind's a little subsystem, and the game is much more interesting than that, much more interesting.

> *I'd rather have my heartbreak again and again, moment by moment, because then I am alive...*

I mean, I live in a world, and this is hard to hear, I live in a world where, even though I don't ask for it, I'm not a masochist, but the sufferings that I undergo become the grace of the opportunity to purify. And I can say suffering is grace, and it hurts like hell and it stinks, but it is still grace. *It is still grace.*

LOVING AWARENESS

When talking about awareness, most of us identify with our awareness through the ego, through the mind and senses. But the true self is in the middle of our chest, in our spiritual heart. So, to get from ego to the true self I said, "I am loving awareness."

Loving awareness is the soul. I am loving awareness. I am aware of everything, I'm aware of my body and my senses and my mind, I'm aware of all of it, but I notice that I'm loving all of it. I'm loving all of the world. The self that I identify with emanates from the ocean of love. The self that is the ego is the ocean of fear. When I am loving awareness I'm aware of everything outside, but pulling into the heart, the spiritual heart, brings me to loving awareness. I'm aware of my thoughts, but loving awareness is simply witnessing them.

> *Only this moment is real...this moment of loving awareness. The past and the future are all just thoughts.*

Loving awareness is in the moment. I have thoughts about the past and future, and those are not helpful, so I dive deep into the present and the presence and in this present moment we will find loving awareness. Only this moment is real, this moment of loving awareness. The past and the future are all just thoughts.

In this spiritual heart there is peace, there is contentment, and there is compassion. There is also joy and wisdom, all inside of your spiritual heart and mine. So when you say, "I want a peaceful world," you don't look outside, you go inside where peace exists.

In Hinduism there is a story about a horse drawn carriage. The horseman who is on top of the carriage represents the ego, and the spiritual heart or the soul is in the carriage. The horses represent your motivation, and anytime the soul decides that the horse is going the wrong way, the soul takes his stick and taps on the window and tells the horseman to go in a different direction.

So most of us identify with the horseman, because you are an incarnation that includes the ego. The soul has come from many previous incarnations, it's been through many births and deaths and it has no fear. The ego is afraid that when this incarnation is ended, it's all going to end. The soul knows that he or she goes through incarnation after incarnation. Your incarnation includes your parents, your body, your friends, your culture. I am in this body – this body, my personality, are all in time and space, but I am not in time or space. I am infinite. I am loving awareness.

I move as Thou movest me; I speak as Thou makest me speak. — Ramakrishna

First God, then cha... doing good to others, doing good to the ... redeeming people. — Sri Ramakrishna

Reformers ha... the ancient Smritis ... Mah.

MEDITATION

AN INTRODUCTION TO MEDITATION

Meditation is basic spiritual practice for quieting the mind and getting in touch with our deeper Self, the spirit. Meditation provides a deeper appreciation of the interrelatedness of all things and the part each person plays. The simple rules of this game are honesty with yourself about where you are in your life and learning and listening to hear how it is. Meditation is a way of listening more deeply, so you hear how it all is from a more profound place. Meditation enhances your insight, reveals your true nature, and brings you inner peace.

A meditation practice is extremely useful in clearing stuff away and letting you see how your mind keeps creating your universe. The ego will keep you occupied with its endless story line of thought forms. Just keep watching them until they dissolve.

Most traditions require a regular practice in order to progress, to get ahead. On the other hand, there are traditions in which no regular practice is required and people do fine, so I can't say it is necessary. But I certainly find it useful, and I encourage other people to do it.

Regularly practicing meditation, even when you don't feel like it, will help you see how your thoughts impose limits and color your existence. Resistances to meditation are your mental prisons in miniature.

It's delicate, because you have to practice from the place of really remembering why you're doing it, with some joy and appreciation. If you go into it with, "Oh, I gotta do my practice," the practice will eventually clean that resistance out of you, but I don't necessarily feel that's a good thing. That's what happens to people when they have to go to church every Sunday. I would rather push you away from spiritual practices until you're so hungry for them that you really want to do a practice, rather than give you a sense that you ought to do the practice or that you're a bad person if you don't do it, because you will end up hating the whole business. In the long run I don't think it will be good for you. Spiritual practice is wonderful if you want to do it. And if you don't, don't.

SHIFTING OUR PERSPECTIVE WITH MEDITATION

Though you can start meditation at any time, it's harder if your life is chaotic, and if you're feeling paranoid, if you're overwhelmed with responsibilities, or if you're sick. But even starting under these conditions, meditation will help you to clear things up a bit. Slowly you reorganize your life to support your spiritual journey; at each stage there will be something you can do to create a supportive space. It may mean changing your diet, who you're with, how you spend your time, what's on your walls, what books you read, what you fill your consciousness with, how you care for your body, or where and how you sit to meditate. All these factors contribute to the depth and freedom that you can know through meditation.

You are under no pressure to rush these changes. You need not fear that because of meditation you are going to lose control and get swept away by a new way of life. As you gradually develop a quiet and clear awareness, your living habits will naturally come into harmony with your total environment, with your past involvements, present interests, and future concerns. There need be no sudden ending of relationships in order to prove your holiness. Such frantic changes only show your own lack of faith. When you are one in truth, in the flow, the changes in your life will come naturally.

You start cleaning up your life when you feel that you can't go on until you do. Cleaning up your life means extricating yourself from those things that are obstacles to your liberation. But keep in mind that nothing in and of itself is an obstacle; it's your attachment to it or your motive for doing it that is the obstacle. It's not an issue of eating meat or not eating meat; it's who's eating it and why.

If your senses can be caught and held by something, you are still chained to the world. It's your attachment to the objects of your senses that imprisons you. Failing to break off the attachments of the senses ultimately holds you back. The minute you aren't preoccupied with what's out there, then that pull is lost. You are free to go deep in meditation.

It's not easy. It's a stinker to get to that level of purity. You start out with things like what you eat, who you sleep with, what you watch on TV, what you do with your time. Many people fool themselves and imitate someone else's purity. They do it in an imitative way, one of fear of being unholy. Abstaining from something for the wrong reason is no better than doing it. You can't pretend to be pure; you can only go at your own speed.

As changes occur through meditation you find yourself attracted to things that are inconsistent with your old model of who you are. Usually, for example, after having meditated in a rigorous (and somewhat righteous) fashion, I have then taken time off to wallow in television, go to movies, take baths and relax. Then, to my surprise, I found myself not being attracted as much as before to these diversions, but being pulled toward just sitting quietly. This new way of being didn't fit with my model of who I was. It was as if I were living with somebody I didn't know very well. My models of myself hadn't changed fast enough to keep up with who I was becoming.

MEDITATION AND EXPECTATIONS

When you begin to meditate you may notice changes right away. You may feel less anxious or more alert. You may be better able to concentrate, have more energy, be more at ease socially, or be more powerful intellectually. Or nothing much may seem to change. Don't count on anything dramatic. Most changes happen slowly.

There is a wide variety of experiences you will have during meditation itself, such as feelings of a pleasant calmness, a slight exhilaration, or, if you're fatigued, strong drowsiness. A common report is the feeling of the mind speeding up. Actually, this is not what is happening, but rather your awareness is standing back a bit so that for the first time you notice the normal speediness of your thoughts. Other kinds of experiences can include seeing images with your eyes closed, hearing inner sounds, or having inner smells, tastes, or new sensations in the body; these are less common. Outside meditation, you may find a sense of spaciousness in your life, a new peace.

All of these experiences, because of their novelty, have a great fascination. But they are best seen as markers along the way, signposts to be noticed, read, perhaps enjoyed, and then left behind as you go on.

There is no "best" or "right" kind of experience in meditation; each session is as different and unique as each day of your life.

If you have ideas of what should happen, you can become needlessly disappointed if your meditation doesn't conform to these expectations. At first meditation is likely to be a novel, and it's easy to feel you are changing. After a while, there may be fewer dramatically novel experiences, and you may feel you're not making any progress. In fact, you may be making the most "progress" when you don't feel anything particularly significant is going on – the changes you undergo in meditation are often too subtle to detect accurately. Suspend judgment and let whatever comes come and go.

It's not easy. It's a stinker to get to that level of purity.

Some people find meditation boring. They feel as if nothing is happening. This is another way in which the old you holds on tight; and it is important to be able to persist even through the experiences of boredom. Set yourself a period of time to seriously try meditation, perhaps a period of two weeks or a month in which you say to yourself, "No matter what I experience in meditation I will continue to do it regularly." This will give you a chance to get through discouraging experiences in meditation such as boredom. On the other hand, the initial reaction to meditation may be just the opposite of boredom – ecstasy.

Many people find things happening after their first few meditative experiences that give them incredible enthusiasm and truly ecstatic states. This may lead them to proselytize, to want to tell others. I suggest that in the early stages you move gently and slowly. Don't overreact.

Positive experiences may well be followed shortly after by indifference. If you don't keep your experiences to yourself you may find yourself caught in a social situation in which you have created a monster of enthusiasm

An evening with RAM DASS

SUNDAY NIGHT, JUNE 7th at 7:30
HUMBOLDT STATE UNIVERSITY, EAST GYM

Tickets, $5.00. Outlets: *Arcata,* Northtown Books and H.S.U., Nelson Hall Ticket Office. *Eureka,* Osiris Books. *Fortuna,* Fortuna Natural Foods. *Garberville,* Shooting Star Textiles. Tickets also available *at the door.* *Out of town,* advance ticket sales write to: Barbara Nielsen, 2170 Western Ave., Arcata, CA 95521.

For further information contact: Linda Devi (707) 677-0318.

full circle

that you must pump up in a false way in order to be consistent. It is wise in all stages of meditation to be calm and not to make too much of any of your experiences, positive or negative. Merely notice them and keep on with your meditation.

Some people overreact to their experiences and go around saying they're enlightened – they're the Buddha, they're the Christ. This is a self-deception. Others go to the other extreme and say they are nothing, they are unworthy. Both these positive and negative attitudes have to go.

Be open to whatever experiences come in your meditation. Don't get fixated on a model of what meditation is supposed to feel like. Set aside judging, being critical, having opinions. Meditation is giving up models and labels.

The less you expect, the less you judge, the less you cling to this or that experience as significant, the further you will progress. For what you're seeking is a transformation of your being far beyond that which any specific experience can give you. It is important to expect nothing, to take every experience, including the negative ones, as merely steps on the path, and to proceed.

MEDITATION IN ACTION

To integrate meditation into your awareness is to use the stuff of daily life as part of your meditation. There are ways of perceiving the world and the way you live in it such that each experience brings you more deeply into the meditative space. At the same time, however, this kind of meditation requires firm grounding: you must continue to function effectively in the world as you meditate on it. This is meditation in action. It finally becomes the core of a consciously lived life, a meditative space within you. This space stands between each thing you notice and each response you make, allowing a peaceful, quiet, and spacious view of the universe.

I find that even an act as stimulating as walking through New York City can be a profound meditative experience. For as I walk down the street, if I stay quiet inside – either through mantra or watching my breath – I can see my consciousness being pulled this way and that by the things along the street. Each time my consciousness is pulled, it reflects some desire system, such as desire for power or sex, to which I am still attached. Each time I notice this, I let it be, let it stay or leave as it chooses. As I do, I remain in the meditative space, not getting lost in the desire. In this way I can walk through the city, staying quiet inside, despite the incredible panoply of stimuli that impinges upon my every sense.

There are techniques that help you see moment-to-moment experiences in such a way that everything serves to awaken you. The Bhagavad Gita describes karma yoga as the path of awakening through ordinary activities. You see every action, be it eating, sleeping, marrying, or earning a living, as an act offered to God. Your every act becomes a meditation on your relation to God. If your path is through the guru, then you see each daily life experience as part of a dialogue in which the guru keeps facing you with experience after experience, each one designed for your awakening.

When you finally develop the capacity to meditate from the moment of awakening to the moment of sleep, and yet stay perfectly at ease in the world, moment-to-moment living becomes a totally delightful and freeing experience.

A MEDITATION ON THE GURU

Imagine a realized being standing before you, someone to whom you feel particularly attuned, such as Christ, Mary, Mohammad, Ram, Hanuman, Anandamayi Ma, or your guru. This being is radiant, luminous, with eyes that are filled with compassion. You feel this being radiating the wisdom that comes from an intimate harmony with the universe.

It is just so incredibly gentle and beautiful to start a dialogue of love with a being who is love. Sit in your meditation area and gaze at a picture of a being whose love is pure, whose love reflects the light of God. Experience that love flowing back and forth between you and the picture. Just open yourself and surrender.

See yourself reflected in those compassionate, non-judging eyes, and allow yourself to open more and more. This is your Beloved. Sit before this being, or imagine such a being sitting in your heart. Just be with that being and return the love. Despite all of the impurities to which you cling, despite all your feelings of unworthiness, such a being loves you unconditionally. It's OK to carry on imaginary conversations with this being; the exchange opens you to compassion, tranquility, warmth, patience—to all the qualities of a free being.

> *And as you become more and more a statement of love, you fall into love with everyone.*

This interpersonal quality of devotional meditation allows you to start from your psychological need to love and to be loved and to bring it into the presence of wisdom, compassion, and peace. When you are with a being who embodies these qualities, they rub off, and you feel more evolved, even to the point of recognizing the radiant light within yourself. Acknowledging your own beauty allows you to open even more to the Beloved, until finally the lover and Beloved merge, and you find that what you had seen outwardly as perfection in your Beloved is a mirror of your own inner beauty.

Ultimately you become that kind of love. You're living in that space and don't need anybody to turn you on to love because you are it, and everybody that comes near you drinks of it. And as you become more and more the statement of love, you fall into love with everyone.

MANTRA AND MEDITATION

You go equipped with mala beads out into the world. The beads and the mantra are like a thread that connects you right to Maharajji's heart. *Shri Ram, Jai Ram, Jai Jai Ram. Om Namah Shivaya.* You can do *Ram, Ram, Ram, Ram*.

You have visualization meditations and you have meditations on breath and meditations on how to become mindful of the moment. If I have one sense of the method that is the base of the whole spiritual game, it's meditation practice, sitting for 20 minutes once or twice a day.

Set aside your work, your letters, your telephone calls, all the other stuff. You might have to wait till the kids to go to bed. No television, no music, just sit. Keep quieting the mind a little bit. Either pick one image like silence or compassion and play with it, or visualize yourself with a Buddha in your heart. Or follow your breath. If you get tired, get up and do a walking meditation around your room.

Don't miss the opportunity to meditate. It purifies, lightens, clears. It gets rid of all the stuff each day if done a couple of times a day. Beautiful. It'll clean out your system like a good tonic.

Unconditional Love

LOVE FOR NO REASON

Unconditional love really exists in each of us. It is part of our deep inner being. It is not so much an active emotion as a state of being. It's not "I love you" for this or that reason, not "I love you if you love me." It's love for no reason, love without an object. It's just sitting in love, a love that incorporates the chair and the room and permeates everything around. The thinking mind is extinguished in love.

If I go into the place in myself that is love and you go into the place in yourself that is love, we are together in love. Then you and I are truly in love, the state of being love. That's the entrance to Oneness. That's the space I entered when I met my guru.

Years ago in India I was sitting in the courtyard of the little temple in the Himalayan foothills. Thirty or forty of us were there around my guru, Maharajji. This old man wrapped in a plaid blanket was sitting on a plank bed, and for a brief uncommon interval everyone had fallen silent. It was a meditative quiet, like an open field on a windless day or a deep clear lake without a ripple. I felt waves of love radiating toward me, washing over me like a gentle surf on a tropical shore, immersing me, rocking me, caressing my soul, infinitely accepting and open.

I was nearly overcome, on the verge of tears, so grateful and so full of joy it was hard to believe it was happening. I opened my eyes and looked around, and I could feel that everyone else around me was experiencing the same thing. I looked over at my guru. He was just sitting here, looking around, not doing anything. It was just his being, shining like the sun equally on everyone. It wasn't directed at anyone in particular. For him it was nothing special, just his own nature.

This love is like sunshine, a natural force, a completion of what is, a bliss that permeates every particle of existence. In Sanskrit it's called *sat-cit-ananda*, "truth-consciousness-bliss," the bliss of consciousness of existence. That vibrational field of ananda love permeates everything; everything in that vibration is in love. It's a different state of being beyond the mind. We were transported by Maharajji's love from one vibrational level to another, from the ego to the soul level. When Maharajji brought me to my soul through that love, my mind just stopped working. Perhaps that's why unconditional love is so hard to describe, and why the best descriptions come from mystic poets. Most of our descriptions are from the point of view of conditional love, from an interpersonal standpoint that just dissolves in that unconditioned place.

When Maharajji was near me, I was bathed in that love.

OPEN YOUR HEART

It is so incredibly gentle and beautiful to start a dialogue of love with a being who is love.

Some of you have known Meher Baba who is such great love, or Christ who is a statement of love, who is love itself. You just open yourself. You can sit in your little meditation area and you take a picture of a being whose love is pure, whose love is in the light of God. It's not the love of personality, it's not the love of romance, it's not that needful love, "I need you."

Romantic love is jealous and possessive because the object of that relationship becomes your connection to that place in you which is love. The kind of love that Christ gives is conscious, unconditional love. He just is love. And ultimately you become that kind of love. There's no need about it. You're living in that space and don't need anybody to turn you on to love because you are it and everybody that comes near you drinks of it.

And as you become more and more the statement of love, you fall in love with everyone. There's nobody here that I don't feel in love with when I look at them, because all I see is the part of them that is love. I can see all their impediments too, it's all there but I'm not climbing into it. I'm not denying it, but I'm not getting stuck in it either. And because you feel love when you are with me, it opens you to the place in yourself that is love.

Sometimes when you feel that, you want to cling to me because I'm your love connection; but I'm not clingable to. There's no way you can collect me; the only way to do it is to become it yourself. Otherwise you're always going to be looking for connections.

If you follow your heart nothing will happen to you, you are protected. As long as your actions are based on your pure seeking for God, you are safe. And any time you are unsure or frightened about your situation, there's a beautiful and very powerful mantra that you can repeat to yourself – "The power of God is within me. The grace of God surrounds me." It will protect you. Experience the power of it; it's like a solid steel shaft that goes from above through the top of your head right down to the base of your being. Grace will surround you like a force field. Through an open heart one hears the universe.

BEING LOVE NOW

I honor the light in all of us. The more I love God, the more I love the forms of God, which are all forms. Living from the soul is very much a heart-center journey. I get on a bus, and by the time I get off, I feel like I have met intimately family members I've known all my life. We're all in love with one another. To live in your spiritual heart with the degree of openness it entails, trust in the One. In that loving awareness, you are not as vulnerable as you would be in the ego, where you think you are separate from others.

How does one become loving awareness? If I change my identification from the ego to the soul, then as I look at people, they all appear like souls to me. I change from my head, the thought of who I am, to my spiritual heart, which is a different sort of awareness – feeling directly, intuiting, loving awareness. It's changing from a worldly outer identification to a spiritual inner identification. Concentrate on your spiritual heart, right in the middle of your chest. Keep repeating the phrase, "I am loving awareness. I am loving awareness. I am loving awareness."

The object of our love is love itself. It is the inner light in everyone and everything. Love is a state of being. You begin to love people because they just are. You see the mystery of the Divine in form. When you live in love, you see love everywhere you look. You are literally in love with everyone you look at.

When you and I rest together in loving awareness, we swim together in the ocean of love. Remember, it's always right here. Enter into the flow of love with a quiet mind and see all things with love as part of yourself.

> *The object of our love is love itself. It is the inner light in everyone and everything.*

UNCONDITIONAL LOVE

So I started out on the New York thruway. I was just galumphing along in such a high state that I was hanging out with various forms of the Divine. I was doing my mantra, which I usually am doing one way or another, to remember that this isn't the only game in town. So I'm holding onto the steering wheel and I'm keeping enough consciousness to keep the car on the road. At another part I'm singing to Krishna, who is blue, radiant, and plays the flute. I am in ecstasy hanging out with blue Krishna, driving along the New York freeway, when I noticed in my rear view mirror a blue flashing light.

Now, there is enough of me down, so I knew it was a state trooper. I pulled over the car, and this man got out of the car and he came up to the window. I opened the window and he said, "May I see your license and registration?" I was in such a state that when I looked at him, I saw that it was Krishna who had come to give me darshan. How would Krishna come in 1970? Why not as a state trooper? Christ came as a carpenter.

So Krishna comes up and asks for my license. He can have anything, he can have my life. All he wants is my license and registration. So I give him my license and registration, and it's like throwing flowers at the feet of God. I am looking at him with absolute love.

So he goes back to the car and he calls home. Then he comes back and he walks around the car and he says,

Dear K.K.

If you have listened to your heart (HRIDAYAM) and not your head - you will know that I am always very much with you. I send the love of a brother to you, your brother, sister, cousins and your many essence friends of Naini Tal. At this moment I am listening to the Bhajan that we taped on Christmas eve, 1967.... all about the deers and hunter... that your cousin was so kind to translate. The Sarangi is much treasured and is in a place of honour in my Father's living room. I shall carry it with me wherever I go in the U.S. and shall perhaps find a student of Sarangi who will use and treasure it when I leave to return to Bharat. I shall ask RAM NARAYAN who is a very fine Sarangi player & teacher... now in the U.S... for a suggestion about this.

I have been doing much Shri RAM Jai RAM with the Tamboura. A neurosurgeon from Bombay, Dr Yodh, who plays the Sitar, has helped me to improve my tuning & technique.

No I have not forgotten the record of your Bhajan. Since returning to the U.S. I have spent all the time in a little cabin in the woods on my Father's land & working on the book *From Bindu to Ojas* and doing Sadhana. Twice I went to a big city for a day but found it very difficult. I am not yet far enough along with Sadhana to be able to travel freely in the world and have the worldly things roll off my back like water from the back of a duck. All the seeds of desire (KAM) are not yet cooked. At this point the new young tree still needs to be fenced around. In Bharat you & most others helped me much by respecting Sadhakas. Here in the West there is no such respect and everyone tries to prove that what I am trying to do is nonsense. They are good people but have no idea of the spiritual path. So without Satsang much more difficult..... a true test of the inner fire. And though it go up & down much.... nevertheless in my heart my purpose is clear & firm --- all due to the divine Sharan of Maharaj-ji who I feel to be with me much. I love Him so much that sometime it is hard not rushing back to His lotus feet. But that is only the body. The Spirit of Maharaj-ji is here inside.. and I feel His Ashirbad and so I see this visit to the West as a necessary part of the Sadhana.

I correspond much with Chota Maharaj-ji who is now living alone in jungle as he wished to do. Bhagawan Dass is perhaps in Sikkhim. I have not heard.

Please tell Kameer Dass that I love him much & that he will still get the pictures. I have had no money yet since coming to the U.S. for making pictures or records or anything. Soon I shall sell the book and then do all the things I promised... including returning to Bharat which is my spiritual home

Please, please touch the feet of Maharaj-ji for me. I want only to serve Him in this life.

So much thought & love to all about you. In the cave of our Heart we are all always present.

Shanti

Ram Dass

"What's in that box on the seat?"

I said, "They're mints, would you like one?"

He said, "Well the problem is you were driving too slow on the freeway, and you'll have to drive off the freeway if you're going to drive this slowly."

I said, "Yes, absolutely." I'm just looking at him with such love.

Now, if you put yourself in the role of a state trooper, how often do you suppose they are looked at with unconditional love? Especially when they're in their uniform. So after he had finished all the deliberations, he didn't want to leave. But he had run out of state trooper-ness. So he stood there a minute, and then he said, "Great car you've got here!" That allowed me to get out. And we could kick and spit and hit the fenders, and say stuff like they don't make `em now like they used to, and tell old car stories. Then we ran out of that.

I could feel he still didn't want to leave. I mean, why would you want to leave if you're being unconditionally loved? Where are you going to go? You've already got what you wanted. What are you going to do? That takes care of your power needs, all of it. So finally he runs out, he knows he's got to come clean that he's Krishna, so he says, "Be gone with you." Which really isn't state trooper talk, but what the hell.

As I get into the car and I start to drive away, he's standing by his cruiser and I look in the mirror and he's waving at me. Now you tell me, do you think that was a state trooper, or was that Krishna? I don't know.

OCEAN OF DEVOTION

Once you have drunk from the water of unconditional love, no other well can satisfy your thirst. The pangs of separation may become so intense that seeking the affection of the Beloved becomes an obsession. When we were with Maharajji, we were intoxicated with his form, the colors of his blanket, the buttery softness of his skin, his tapering, almost simian fingers, the long eyelashes that so often hid his eyes, the red toenail on his big toe. As with any lover we, too, became fascinated and enamored of every detail, although these cues triggered spiritual bliss instead of physical desire.

> *Once you experience unconditional love, you really get hooked.*

In their way intoxication and addiction are analogies for devotion. Once you experience unconditional love, you really get hooked. The attraction is to that intimacy between the lover and the Beloved.

You are so drawn into the songs, stories, images and constant remembrance of the Beloved that you may hold on to the form and not want to go on to the next stage. You are always thinking about it and tuning your being to stay in that intimate loving relationship with this person you love.

But the Beloved is not a person in the usual sense, and the form is just a costume for the play, the lila. Ultimately, this form is the one that takes you beyond form. What the Beloved, your guru, reveals to you is your own soul. Even so you may choose like Hanuman, to remain in a kind of duality to serve and remain immersed in the ocean of devotion.

The devotional path isn't necessarily a straight line to enlightenment. There's a lot of back and forth, negotiations if you will, between the ego and the soul. You look around at all the aspects of suffering, and you watch your heart close in judgment. Then you practice opening it again and loving this too, as a manifestation of the Beloved, another way the Beloved is taking form. Again your love grows vast. In Bhakti, as you contemplate, emulate, and take on the qualities of the Beloved, your heart keeps expanding until you see the whole universe as the Beloved, even the suffering.

As I have explored my own and others' journeys toward love, I've encountered different types of happiness. There's pleasure, there's happiness, and then there's joy. Addiction, even in the broad sense of just always wanting more of something, gives only pleasure. Pleasure is very earthbound when you're getting it from sensual interaction, and it always has its opposite; also, the need for satisfaction is never ending. Happiness is emotional, and emotions come and go. It may play into the complex of other emotional stuff that we all carry. But there is also spiritual happiness, which gets very close to joy.

As it becomes less personal, spiritual happiness becomes joy. Joy is being part of the One. It's spiritual, the joy-full universe, like trees are joyful. It's bliss, or ananda. It's all those things. The difference is that it comes from the soul.

BEING LOVE

The most important aspect of love is not in giving or the receiving: it's in the being. When I need love from others, or need to give love to others, I'm caught in an unstable situation. Being in love, rather than giving or taking love, is the only thing that provides stability. Being in love means seeing the Beloved all around me.

I'm not interested in being a "lover." I'm interested in only being love. In our culture we think of love as a relational thing: "I love you" and "you are my lover." But while the ego is built around relationship, the soul is not. It wants only to be love.

It's a true joy, for example, to turn someone whom you didn't initially like into the Beloved. One way I practice doing so is by placing a photograph of a politician with whom I intensely disagree on my puja table – my altar. Each morning when I wake up, I say good morning to the Buddha, to my guru, and to the other holy beings there. But I find that it's with a different spirit that I say, "Hello Mr. Politician." I know it sounds like a funny thing to do, but it reminds me of how far I have to go to see the Beloved in everybody.

Being love is a supreme creative act.

Mother Teresa has described this as "seeing Christ in all his distressing disguises." When I realized that Mother Teresa was actually involved in an intimate love affair with each and every one of the poor and the lepers she was picking up from the gutters in India, I thought to myself, " That's the way to play the game of love." And that is what I have been training myself for the last past quarter century: to see and be with the Beloved everywhere.

One of the interesting aspects of seeing the Beloved in this way is that it doesn't require the other person to see him – or herself as the Beloved. All that's necessary is that I focus on my own consciousness properly. It's interesting to notice, though, how warmly people respond to being seen as the Beloved, even if they don't know what's happening. Of course, it all assumes that all your feelings are genuine and that you aren't compelled to act on them or to lay any sort of trip on the other person. The idea is simply to live and breathe among the Beloved.

The way I work at seeing others (like the politician), as the Beloved is to remind myself, "This is another soul, just like me, who has taken a complicated incarnation, just as I have. I don't want to be in this incarnation any more than he wants to be in mine. But since I want to rest in my soul and not in my ego, I would like to give everybody the opportunity to do the same."

If I can see the soul that happens to have incarnated into a person that I don't care for, then my consciousness becomes an environment in which he or she is free to come up from air if he or she wants to. That person can do so because I'm not trying to keep him or her locked into being the person that he or she has become. It's liberating to resist another person politically, yet still see him or her as another soul. That's what Krishna meant when he said, "I'm not going to fight, because they are all my cousins on the side." We may disagree with one another in our current incarnation, but we are all souls.

When you see the Beloved all around you, everyone is family and everywhere is love. When I allow myself to really see the beauty of another being, to see the inherent beauty of soul manifesting itself, I feel the quality of love in that beings presence. It doesn't matter what we're doing. We could be talking about our cats because we happen to be picking out cat food in the supermarket, or we simply could be passing each other on the sidewalk. When we are being love, we extend outward an environment that allows people to act in different, more loving and peaceful ways than they are used in behaving. Not only does it allow them to be more loving, it encourages them to be so.

In 1969 I was giving a series of lectures in New York City. Every night, taking the bus up Third Avenue, I got the same extraordinary bus driver. Every night it was rush hour in one of the busiest cities in the world, but he had a warm word and a caring presence for each person who got on the bus. He drove us as if he were sculling a boat down a river, flowing through the traffic rather than resisting it. Everyone who got on the bus was less likely to kick the dog that evening or to be otherwise hostile and unloving, because of the loving space that driver had created. Yet all he was doing was driving the bus. He wasn't a therapist or a great spiritual teacher. He was simply being love.

Remember, we are all affecting the world every moment, whether we mean to or not. Our actions and states of mind matter, because we are so deeply interconnected with one another. Working on our own consciousness is the most important thing that we are doing at any moment, and being love is a supreme creative act.

RELATIONSHIP

THE PREDICAMENT OF LOVING

This is the path of love. The path of the heart. Like all paths, it is fraught with pitfalls and traps, and most of our emotions are either in the service of our minds or our frightening things that overwhelm us and make us afraid so we protect ourselves from them.

So we come through life a little bit like hungry ghosts. We are beings that have huge needs for love, but seemingly it's like we have some kind of amoeba that doesn't allow us to digest our food. So, though we get love, it goes through us and then we need love all over again. This conception is so deep within all of us that we've built an entire reality around it, and we think that's the way it is; that everybody needs love and that if you don't get it you are deprived, and that the more of it the better, and you need it every day from everything. In that sense it's like an achievement; you see people that are achievers. The minute they achieve something it becomes irrelevant, and their awareness turns to the next achievement because they are addicted to the practice, not to the goal.

The predicament with loving is the power of the addiction of the practice of loving somebody; of getting so caught in the relationship that you can't ever arrive at the essence of dwelling in love.

THE TRIANGLE

The image I always had when performing a wedding was the image of a triangle.

One in which there are the two partners, and a third force. This third force is that which emerges out of the interaction of these two partners. It is the shared awareness that lies behind the two of them. They are in this yoga of a relationship and have come together as one, in order to find the shared awareness that exists behind them, allowing them to then dance as two so that the twoness brings them into one and the oneness dances as two. That is the kind of vibrating relationship between the one and the two, so that people are both separate and yet they are not separate.

But often, we come into a relationship very much identified with our needs at some level or other. "I need security, I need refuge, I need friendship." We come together because we fulfill each other's needs at some level and the problem is that when you identify with that, those needs, you always stay at the level where the other person is "her" or "him" that is satisfying that need. It really only gets extraordinarily beautiful when it becomes "us" and then goes behind the "us" and becomes "one."

YOGA OF RELATIONSHIPS

To enter into the yoga of relationship is the hardest yoga that I know of actually, because your ego is so vulnerable when you start to open up to another human being. And before that one place gets going strong enough, you get frightened and you pull back and you get entrenched and that happens all the time in relationships. People that come together with the greatest meaning of feeling love and then they get caught in their needs and their frustrations and they separate.

One of the problems is that we tend to place relationships a little bit on the back burner in life. We get a relationship and then we go out to a job and we go out to other things. Now that we have that together, we go do life. And for a relationship to be a yoga of relationship is like a full time operation for years. For me, one of my examples is Stephen and Ondrea Levine.

Stephen and Ondrea used to be really nice, friendly, sociable people – before they met. And then they met and they really started to be together and the amount of energy that had to go into staying clear with each other was profound. Because what happens is so much goes down so fast in relationships, it's really hard to process it fast enough to keep clear. So you keep getting this kind of residual of old stuff that isn't quite digested enough and you

end up separate from the person because you didn't have time to stop and kind of work it through, clear it, and so on.

So what they did was they moved on to land with no telephone. Put up a big sign, "No Trespassing." And they just started to work with one another. And after some years, during which you really felt like you were cut off as a friend, they began to open up to me and allow me in and then I began to see the effect of that. I began to see what happens when people learn how to really open, trust, meditate together, keep emptying, keep clearing, and work until they are a shared awareness.

It's not fair to say that any relationship that isn't involved in the yoga of relationship is not useful and fulfilling to people. A lot of people come together because it is just really comfortable living with another person and there is a wonderful kind of sweet intimacy. And it's fun to cook with each other and to sleep together and it's fun to just live life together without trying to get too deep in as a spiritual practice. And many of those people have other spiritual practices. They go off and meditate and one does something else – Tai Chi or something else. And that seems fine to me. I don't think you should make believe that a relationship is really yoga unless you are willing to really put the effort into making it such. And if you are, it really fills all the space for a long time.

> All of us here are one in drag, appearing to be many. So we are all "soul mates."

THE IDEA OF SOUL MATES

All of us here are one in drag, appearing to be many. So we are all "soul mates." And it's not really mates, because it's not even two. It's only one. There's only one of us. So what you're really doing is constantly marrying yourself at the deepest level of God marrying God.

Now you come down into soul. And each soul has a unique karmic predicament (you could call it a psychic DNA code) that in a way guides which way its life will go. And it is entirely possible that souls, when they take birth into parents that are part of their karma, will at some point meet a being and they have agreed in advance to come down and do this together and meet. And that's what we usually call soul mates.

What you have found from your past relationships and marriages is that what you are attracted to in a person isn't what you ultimately live with. After the honeymoon is over —after the desire systems that carry the attraction have passed — then you are left with the work to do. And it's the same work. When you trade in one partner for another, you still have the same work. You're going to have to do it sooner or later when the pizzazz is over. And you can't milk the romanticism of relationship too long as you become more conscious. It's more interesting than that. It really is.

People keep wanting to romanticize their lives all the time. It's part of the culture. But the awakening process starts to show you the emptiness of that forum. And you start to go for something deeper. You start to go to meet another human being in truth. And truth is scary. Truth has bad breath at times; truth is boring; truth burns the food; truth is all the stuff. Truth has anger; truth has all of it. And you stay in it and you keep working with it and your keep opening to it and you keep deepening it.

But you begin to see how you keep coming to the same place in relationships, and then you tend to stop. Because it gets too heavy. Because your identity gets threatened too much. For the relationship to move to the next level of truth requires an opening and a vulnerability that you're not quite ready to make. And so you entrench, you retrench, you pull back and then you start to judge and push away and then you move to the next one.

And then you have the rush of the openness and then the same thing starts to happen. And so you keep saying "Where am I going to find the one when this doesn't happen?" And it will only happen when it doesn't happen in you. When you start to take and watch the stuff and get quiet enough inside yourself, so you can take that process as it's happening and start to work with it. And keep coming back to living truth in yourself or the other person even though it's scary and hard.

KARMA AND RELATIONSHIPS

When I am in a relationship with somebody else, and what they do upsets me; because I understand that my life experiences are the gift of my Guru in order to bring me to God, if somebody upsets me, that's my problem. This is a hard one, because we don't usually think these ways in this culture.

What I see other people as is trees in the forest. You go to the woods and you see gnarled trees and live oaks and pines and hemlocks and elms and things like that. And you are not inclined to say, "I don't like you because you are a pine and not an elm." You appreciate trees the way they are.

But the minute you get near humans, you notice how quick it changes. It's a way in which you don't allow humans to just manifest the way they are. You take it personally. You keep taking other people personally. All they are is mechanical run-offs of old karma. Really, it's what they are. I mean they look real and they think they are real, but really what they are is mechanical run-off. So they say, "Grrrh!" And you karmically go, "Grrrh!" And then one of you says, "We've got to work this out." And the other says, "Yes, we must." And then you start to work it out. It's all mechanical. It's all condition stuff.

So somebody comes along and gets to me. They get me angry or uptight or they awaken some desire in me, wow, am I delighted. They got me. And that's my work on myself. If I am angry with you because your behavior doesn't fill my model of how you should be, that's my problem for having models. No expectations, no upset. If you are a liar and a cheat, that's your karma. If I'm cheated, that's my work on myself.

My attempting to change you, that's a whole other ballgame. What I am saying is if I will only be happy if you are different than you are, you are asking for it. You are really asking for it. Think of how many relationships you say, "I really don't like that person's this or that. If they would only be this. If I could manipulate them to be this, I can be happy." Isn't that weird? Why can't I be happy with them the way they are? You are a liar, a cheat and a scoundrel and I love you. I won't play any games with you, but I love you. It's interesting to move to the level where you can appreciate, love, and allow in the same way you would in the woods. Instead of constantly bringing in that judging component which is really rooted out of your own feelings of lack of power. Judging comes out of your own fear. Now I fall trap to it all the time. But every time I do, I catch myself.

I think in relationships, you create an environment with your own work on yourself, which you offer to another human being to use to grow in the way they need to grow. You keep working – you become the soil – moist and soft and receptive so the person can grow the way they need to grow, because how do you know how they should grow?

> ...if somebody upsets me, that's my problem.

> What I see other people as is trees in the forest. You go to the woods and you see gnarled trees and live oaks and pines and hemlocks and elms and things like that. And you are not inclined to say, "I don't like you because you are a pine and not an elm." You appreciate trees the way they are.

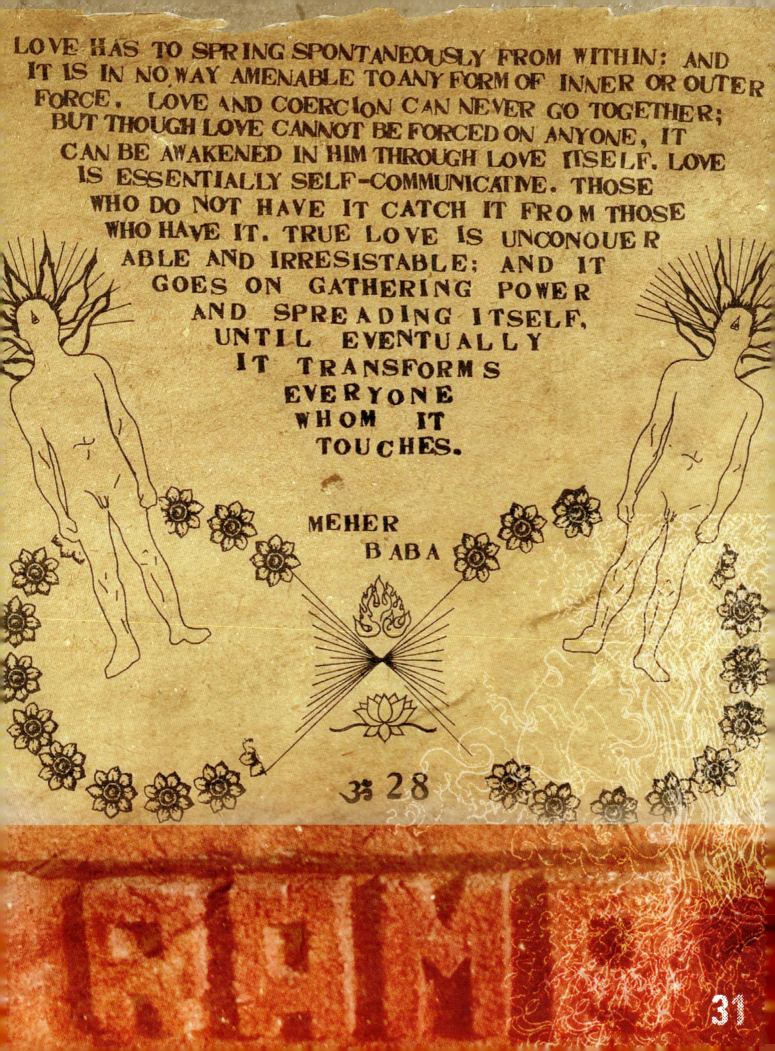

LOVE HAS TO SPRING SPONTANEOUSLY FROM WITHIN; AND IT IS IN NO WAY AMENABLE TO ANY FORM OF INNER OR OUTER FORCE. LOVE AND COERCION CAN NEVER GO TOGETHER; BUT THOUGH LOVE CANNOT BE FORCED ON ANYONE, IT CAN BE AWAKENED IN HIM THROUGH LOVE ITSELF. LOVE IS ESSENTIALLY SELF-COMMUNICATIVE. THOSE WHO DO NOT HAVE IT CATCH IT FROM THOSE WHO HAVE IT. TRUE LOVE IS UNCONQUERABLE AND IRRESISTABLE; AND IT GOES ON GATHERING POWER AND SPREADING ITSELF, UNTIL EVENTUALLY IT TRANSFORMS EVERYONE WHOM IT TOUCHES.

MEHER BABA

SERVICE and COMPASSIONATE ACTION

FACING YOUR FEARS & SUFFERING

Suffering seems to be a fact of life. How do we face it? Clearly it is a stranger to none of us. Perhaps we've not experienced the corrosive pain of illness, persecution, starvation, or violence. We may not have lived with the deterioration and loss of a loved one. Few of us have seen the charred face of a burned child. But each of us has experienced our fair share of not getting what we want or having to deal with what we don't want. In this, we all know suffering.

The way in which we deal with suffering has much to do with the way in which we are able to be of service to others. Of course, not all helping revolves around suffering. Much of what we offer may be in the nature of simple support or guidance: moving a friend's new furniture, teaching a child to read. But it is the affliction of others that most directly awakens in us the desire to be of care and comfort.

The impulse to do all we can to relieve another's pain is the automatic response of our native compassion. But the experience of suffering — in ourselves and in others — triggers off complicated reactions. To investigate these is itself an act of compassion, an essential step toward becoming more effective instruments of mutual support and healing. How then do we respond to the pain we see all around us? And, once we have investigated this response, how do we respond to our own afflictions?

WHAT IS COMPASSION?

Compassion is a quality of being in relationship to others in the intensity of their lives; it's an appreciation of their lives. The way we usually use it, compassion has to do with the suffering of others, and kindness and gentleness and empathy and "going outward" to another person. But it's actually a more profound spiritual issue than that.

I've been working for a long time with the phrase, "out of emptiness arises compassion," because most of the time when we think of compassion, we think of empathy: we think of seeing suffering and then we want to do something about it. We are concerned and feel for the other person's suffering. But the compassion that one looks at from a spiritual point of view is the kind in which those qualities are balanced with an appreciation of the planes of reality that lie behind what is apparent or obvious. So compassion involves a certain kind of attention or a certain kind of a paradox. For example, when you respond from your human heart's point of view to another person's suffering—when you see a Guatemalan widow, or you see a family lost in crack, or the Chinese students in front of a tank, or what happened to the people around Chernobyl, or something like that—you experience incredible pain in your heart . . . when your heart is open.

Many people just respond with their intellect when they get in the presence of suffering. They can't handle it, so they pull back into their minds and they deal with it intellectually. But if you keep your heart open, it hurts like hell; it really hurts when you can't intellectually push them away, especially when you've started to appreciate that they are *us* and not *them*.

But there is another level of reality—and this is a much harder one for people to hear—in which there is an unfolding of *karma* for those individuals in which their suffering is their route through to awakening, long term though it may be, and, in that sense, you look at the universe as a set of unfolding laws. You see that there are no errors on that plane. You see the perfection of it, so that you're faced with the paradox that, on one level of reality, the suffering stinks, but on the other level, it's perfect. To me, compassion is the ability to embrace both of those simultaneously.

ENTER LIGHTLY

If we are to help heal the world, we need to remember that it is a sacred place. Our actions need to be positive statements, reminders that even in the worst times there is a world worth struggling for. We need to find ways to keep the vision alive, to acknowledge but not get caught in the dark side, to remember that even the worst aspects of suffering are only part of the whole picture. We need to enter lightly.

Entering lightly means not ignoring suffering, but treating it gently. We don't want to ignore another's pain, but our becoming depressed or angry about it doesn't relieve it and may increase it. The delicate balance is in allowing ourselves to feel the pain fully, to be sad or angry or hurt by it, but not be so weighted down by it that we are unable to act to relieve it. It is a matter of ends and means again: to create a caring, loving, peaceful world, we need to act with care and love and peace.

It is the continuing work of life: of learning to trust that the universe is unfolding exactly as it should, no matter how it looks to us; learning to appreciate that each of us has a part in nurturing this interconnectedness whole and healing it where it is torn; discovering what our individual contribution can be, then giving ourselves fully to it. Demanding as that sounds, it is what, in the spiritual sense, we are all here for, and compassionate action gives us yet one more opportunity to live it. It is an opportunity to cooperate with the universe, to be part of what the Chinese call the great river of the Tao. It is not a coincidence that Hanuman, who in the Hindu cosmology is called the "embodiment of selfless service," is the son of the wind god; when we give ourselves into becoming fully who we are by doing fully what we do, we experience lightness, we are like kites in wind, we are on the side of the angels, we are entering lightly.

SERVICE IS A CURRICULUM

Service is an endless series of questions, puzzling and insistent. It not only raises questions, it helps to answer them. Service is a curriculum.

In this curriculum, we encounter our own limitations – we have seen how our ego can lock us into narrow self-images, leaving us tentative and hesitant to reach out. Our resistance to pain can lead us to insulate ourselves from suffering. When our hearts do open in empathy, all too often we close down quickly, frightened by the intensity of our feelings; we substitute denial, pity, or other defense mechanisms for the spontaneous response of the heart. Frequently, we find ourselves so identified with our own needs that we tend to treat others as objects to be manipulated toward our own ends. We see how the restlessness of our minds can hinder our ability to listen; we find ourselves at least one thought away from someone else. And when we try to help through social action, we often so identify an opponent as an enemy that we remain locked in a cycle of recrimination. Meanwhile, as the toxicity of these and other hindrances build up, we begin to wear down. We burn out. Helping starts to hurt.

Entering lightly means not ignoring suffering, but treating it lightly.

But the curriculum of service provides us with information about our strengths as well, and we discover how these contribute to genuinely help-full service. Each time we drop our masks and meet heart-to-heart, reassuring one another simply by the quality of our presence, we experience a profound bond, which we intuitively understand is nourishing everyone.

Each time we quiet our mind, our listening becomes sharp and clear, deep and perceptive; we realize that we know more than we thought we knew, and can reach out and hear, as if from inside, the heart of someone's pain.

Each time we are able to remain open to suffering, despite our fear and defensiveness, we sense a love in us which becomes increasingly unconditional.

KARMA YOGA AND SERVICE

How can the way I serve be a vehicle for my getting free of my own entrapment and my own separateness? In Hinduism, that begins what is called *karma yoga*, meaning "union" or coming to oneness through karma, through the stuff of life, which you use in order to come back to the one.

> Through the act of service you get closer to a place of equanimity in your being.

You can see the difference between the way in which you do an act when you are busy being separate, and the way you do an act when you are separate but attempting to return to the one. The way in which you do the act and how the act affects you changes.

Many images—of Mother Teresa, of Krishna speaking to Arjuna in the Bhagavad Gita—are really concerned with this form of getting closer to the one, to the spirit, or to God, or to unity, or to pure awareness. Through the act of service you get closer to a place of equanimity in your being, a place from which you do the perfect action. If you can hear this, you are doing service for a very different reason. It's still an ego thing, it's still you as somebody doing something, but you are starting as a separate entity and you're doing it in order to come back to a unity experience.

You meet in committees, each with your separate opinions, attitudes, and vested interests in those opinions and attitudes. But in the process, at moments you start to see yourself as separate from your opinions and attitudes and the unity experience of the group starts to be felt. It starts to vie with your holding to your attitude and opinions. Very often there's a little flip of balance where it's less important that you be right then that you be part of the collective consciousness.

You begin to understand the possibility that our collective wisdom is greater than any one individual's wisdom. That's a big shot for most people. Most of us would prefer to think we know best. When we look around, the thought that we would put our lives or our money or anything in trust this way is a risky business. You want a game that awakens you, and that awakening becomes a vehicle that transcends separateness.

You're doing an action now: "I am working to stop nuclear proliferation." Or: "I am working to relieve the suffering of somebody with AIDS." Or: "I am working to help the dolphins." Or: "I am working for whatever purpose." At the same moment, I am working on myself, realizing that until I am free of my identification with my own attitudes, opinions, and separateness, my act of necessity will be perpetuating some degree of divisiveness in the world. Even as I'm doing good, I will also be creating suffering. Knowing that, I've got to work on myself. And I can't stop until I'm enlightened, because the dance goes on and you can't stop acting because you're in an incarnation and the acting just keeps happening. The only conclusion is I will use my actions to work on myself as an offering back into the system. I work on myself as an offering to you; I serve you as a way of working on myself.

That double whammy, or that double investment, or that double process, means that the more you serve, the emptier of identification you get when you're doing karma yoga properly, and the freer of identification of your own separateness you get the more you're being fed. The more you're being fed, the more you can do and the more you want to do. And the more joy you're having from it.

REFLECT ON YOUR MOTIVES

Compassionate action gives us an opportunity to wake up to some of our motives and to act with more freedom. It gives us the chance to put ourselves out on the edge, and if we are willing to take a clean look at what we see there, we can come to know ourselves better. We can't, of course, change what is arising in us at any moment, because we can't change our pasts and our childhoods. But when we listen to our own minds and stop being strangers to ourselves, we increase the number of ways we can respond to what arises. Then we know when we are resisting contact with a poor person because of something that happened in childhood, and we know that now we have nothing to fear either from the homeless person or from the examination of our place in the economic structure.

> We are here right now, and we are free.

We are here right now, and we are free. We can either walk past the person, talk to her, give her some money, and go on, maybe reflecting on the causes of homelessness, or we can cross the street because we are still carrying around fear and protection from childhood and don't want to deal with it today on the way to a meeting.

Whichever we do, with increasing awareness comes an appreciation of our actions as they are, and then they begin to change. Even if we haven't acted compassionately toward the street woman, we haven't repressed the fact that she exists, and we aren't judging ourselves; as awareness and acceptance increase, not blocked by our fears, we tend to act more humanely. It happens naturally.

A central quality in people who are drawn to compassionate action is empathy for those who need help, a commonality with people who are suffering, oppressed or vulnerable. This feeling is often a result of imprinting during childhood, when we had no control over what was happening and felt frightened, helpless, vulnerable, sick and alone in bed on a summer night.

DEALING WITH BURNOUT IN ACTS OF SERVICE

As we struggle against the challenges and frustrations inherent in service, we will find good counsel, many methods, and much support. We can do more than simply struggle to stay afloat; we can discover a more reliable source of continuous buoyancy. We can do more than cope. We can see now that burnout need not always be an enemy. If not a best friend, it can at least be a catalyst, even a guide, for the inner work, the work on ourselves, which is the foundation of all true service, and the only way, finally, to maintain energy and inspiration. If we can view the places where we encounter fatigue and doubt as clues and signposts for that inner work, our journey will not only go more lightly but go further, deeper. We will not simply survive. We will grow.

Meanwhile, it will always serve to stay grounded in humble respect for all that is involved in the work to relieve suffering – a compassion for ourselves which is the source of compassion for all others. Whatever helpful hints for support and freedom we come upon must be tested against daily practice. We will slip and fall again and again. The struggle between heart and mind is fierce and continuous. The need to see suffering relieved is an essential ingredient of our humanity. Inevitably, we will feel the poignancy and despair that arise on those occasions when affliction is not eased; indeed, it grows and spreads, cruel and ominous, despite all our efforts. The pain of the world will sear and break our hearts because we can no longer keep them closed. We've seen too much now. To some degree or other, we have surrendered into service and are willing to pay the price of compassion.

But with it comes the joy of a single, caring act. With it comes the honor of participating in a generous process in which one rises each day and does what one can. With it comes the simple, singular grace of being an instrument of Love, in whatever form, to whatever end.

> *The pain of the world will sear and break our hearts because we can no longer keep them closed.*

USING SERVICE TO REFLECT ON YOURSELF

There are many levels at which you relieve suffering; you relieve suffering at one level by giving food. You relieve suffering at another level by giving the food in such a way that is draws people out of the pain of their own separateness. This involves the idea of respect for the people you're serving, and dignity and really seeing.

You must be driven to work on yourself all of the time, so that your acts of caring for other human beings are not toxic. If you want to help other people, I would say, just look around, maybe check out the bulletin board at your local Laundromat. It doesn't matter where you plug into the system; the issue is the quality of the behavior when you plug into the system.

It's not just doing the act, it's the combination of doing the act with the exercise of using the act to see the ways in which you're ripping off the act for your own psychodynamic needs. Without putting yourself down for it, just appreciating the humanity of it, but also getting to the next level of it, where you're just doing it because you're a part of the dance, and you're on the side of the angels. Gandhi said, "When you surrender completely into God, you find yourself in the service of all that exists."

CREDITS

Awareness
Ram Dass on the beach – Peter Simon
Drawing of Maharaji Shiva Lingum - Roger Loft
Ram Dass and Maharaji - Rameshwar Das
Ram Dass background photo One eye – LSRF Archive
Maharaji in front of Hanuman - LSRF Archive
Ram block print - Adam Bauer
Ram Dass drawing - LSRF Archive
KK/Ram Dass - Rameshwar Das
Ram Dass in crowd - LSRF archive

Meditation
Ram Dass meditating in Van - Peter Simon
Flowers – Raghu Markus
Ram Dass at Lama - LSRF Archive
Evening with Ram Dass poster photo – LSRF Archive
Ram Dass holding flowers - Peter Simon

Unconditional Love
Maharaji with Western girls - Roy Bonney (Krishna Das Yellow)
Maharaji with Hand on His head - Balaram Das
Maharaji smiling on tucket - Roy Bonney
Ganesh – LSRF Archive

Relationship
Ram Dass head shot middle age - LSRF Archive
Ram Dass head on smiling woman - LSRF Archive
Ram Dass with woman and baby - LSRF Archive
Ram Dass hugging two people - LSRF Archive
Kainchi Ashram - LSRF Archives
Be Here Now Book Panel - LSRF Archive

Service and Compassionate Action
Western women in Kainchi with platters of Prasad - Roy Bonney (Krishna Das Yellow)
Ram Dass in Seva t-shirt - Rameshwar Das
Taos Hanuman - NKB Ashram Archive
Ram block print - Adam Bauer
Panel from Love Serve Remember Box set - Gene Gregan
Ram Dass contemporary - Roshi Joan Halifax